WHEN THERE IS NO VISUAL MEANS OF SUPPORT

WHEN THERE IS NO VISUAL MEANS OF SUPPORT

The Secrets Lie Within The Scriptures!
Nuts & Bolts To Survive Life Challenges...

A Memoir

Helen Carter Johnson

MILLIGAN BOOKS, INC.   BOOKS   CALIFORNIA

Published and Distributed:
Milligan Books, Inc.

Cover Design: Kevin Allen
Formatting: Milligan Books

First Printing, January 2009
10987654321

ISBN 978-0-9815783-9-2

Publisher's Note:

Milligan Books, Inc.
1425 W. Manchester Ave., Suite C
Los Angeles, California 90047
Website: www.milliganbooks.com
Telephone: (323) 750-3592

Acknowledgments

To my family and friends:

Thank you for being there for me during my struggles—struggles of letting go of self, procrastination and the 'I don't want to's' in my life. I have finally found the peace that I was meant to have in Christ Jesus.

Helen

Table of Contents

CHAPTER 1

WE ARE NOT ALONE

We were not created to be alone. Even the God Head/Trinity does not operate alone. The disciples asked Jesus to eat, after His encounter with the Samaritan woman at the well. Jesus said unto them, "My meat is to do the will of him that sent me and to finish his work" (St. John 4:34). Again, when Jesus was asked by the Jews if He was the Christ, He answered them, "I told you and you believe me not: the works that I do in my Father's name, they bear witness of me" (St. John 10:25).

In the creation of man, everything that was made had a mate. Male and female, animals, insects, the fowls of the air, all had mates (Genesis 1:25). When God

3

made man from the dust of the ground, He brought every living creature to Adam for him to name (Gen. 2:19-20). God said, "It is not good that the man should be alone; I will make him an help meet for him" (Gen. 2:18).

Furthermore, Moses told God, "I am not able to bear all this people alone." (Num. 11:14-17). When the burden gets too heavy, God sends help. It's the same for us today. When the way gets to rough and the burden gets too heavy, He sends help.

Over 2000 years ago, God sent His only Son, because He saw that man needed a savior. You see, man was not doing well on his own. For thirty years, Jesus was being prepared for His major mission. He was born into this sinful world, through a young virgin girl. He came in the form of a fleshly man, so that He would understand and live as a man. He did so without sin.

The last three years, Jesus prepared His disciples for the job of spreading what He had taught them. He had over seventy disciples, but they slowly left Him. He ended with twelve disciples, and one of them was a devil.

When preparing the apostles for His crucifixion, Jesus let them know that He would leave them a comforter. "But the comforter, which is the Holy Ghost, whom the Father will send in my name, he shall teach you all things and bring all things to your remembrance, whatsoever I have said unto you" (St. John 14:26).

I don't care how bad things may seem, He's there with us and for us. The stress of life comes because we see things in the natural realm and try to fix them ourselves. No matter how bad things look, they are not ours to handle. Tell Jesus about it! He will direct you in all you do. You have to tune your ears to hear what He has to say. Then respond by following, by faith.

We all have roles to play in life. Each part fits together to make up the whole. We each have different callings or gifts. For example, I've been given the gift of helping. For the most part, I listen and encourage. I find that more than anything else, people just want you to listen. They usually know the answer, but need someone to listen (without interruption) to their problems.

Rarely are they looking for advice. Only when they ask for advice, do I give it. This is all part of needing one another. "Not forsaking the assembling of ourselves together, as the manner of some is; but exhorting one another: and so much the more, as you see the day approaching" (Hebrew 10:25). "Let your conversation be without covetousness; and be content with such things as you have: for He has said, I will never leave you nor forsake you" (Hebrew 13:5). It doesn't matter the situation, we are not alone.

Chapter 2

STAY FOCUSED

I have problems staying focused. When cleaning my house, (as well as in other instances), I start out trying to get rid of clothing that I no longer wear. As I separate items, I try on certain pieces to see if they still fit. Before I know it, most of the items are back in the closet. The same thing happens when I go through the file cabinet. How long should I keep warranties and contracts (expired/paid off)? Instead of clearing out things, I just rearrange.

That's sometimes the way we live our lives. Instead of eliminating our clutter, we just rearrange it. So the problem remains the same, just neater. Holding onto the old, leaves no room for the new. It's time to let go of the baggage/clutter in our lives, so God can show us a new thing. Your anger and grudges of the past that you hold on to, are all baggage that should be given to Jesus. He knows how to handle past and present clutter. Looking back can cause stumbling in the present. We cannot go forward, when we have our minds in reverse.

Stay focused on the now. We cannot do anything to correct the past, but we can do something about the present. The enemy wants to keep you from getting what God has in store for you. He camouflages your blessings. He doesn't want you to see the good, so he takes your attention off the prize of the higher calling of God. Don't focus on the problem. Just remember that every problem has a blessing on the other side. Turn your problems over to Jesus and get your blessings. Stay focused! Look beyond the circumstances and remember the promise. "And we know that all things work together for good to them that love

God, to them who are the called according to his purpose" (Romans 8:28).

CHAPTER 3

IT'S TIME TO MOVE ON

There comes a time in your life, when you have to move on. There will be those who you want to come with you, however, you must leave some people behind. The call is on your life and you must answer. We try so hard to make our call be the call for others. Wrong!

Each of us has been put here to do a particular job. If you are not sure what your gift is, seek the answer from the Lord. Most often your gift is something that you have been doing most of your life. It's natural as breathing. You are at your best when you are doing it.

There are times when we don't want to answer the call on our lives. You just don't

15

want the responsibility that goes along with the call. You know you just want to be Momma's baby, even though childhood is 'way out of your reach.' You want to stay where it's safe. You want to hang out at the same playground of protection so someone else can be responsible for you, like when you were a child. Playing in the sandbox of life, you are waiting for someone to pick you up and put your feet through the holes of the baby swing. You want to sit and wait to be pushed.

Even though the style is now straight leg, do you keep looking in your closet, wondering when you will be able to wear those old bell bottom pants? Do you find yourself in the same type of relationship, with the same problems? Do you keep going back to the old neighborhood, even though all your old playmates are grown and gone? God have blessed you with a new house, but you just can't give up that old furniture. It seem to be such a waste to let

16

go of the bed with your body curves that fit perfectly in the sag. Let it go!!! It's time to move on. Women, are you still looking for a mate to take care of you? Get a grip! Your help comes for the Lord (Psalms 121).

I have been given the gifts of servitude and giving. I'm at my best doing those things. I am happiest when I follow the call of my Father. Occasionally, I try to pull others into what I've been called to do. When they won't go willingly, I try to drag them along. Especially, my family. I don't understand why they don't see it my way. Sometimes, I become upset. It's those times that the Lord has to remind me that He did not call my husband, my children, or my friends, to do my job.

I'm reminded of Peter, when Jesus asked him, "Simon, son of Jonas, lovest thou me more than these? He saith unto him, yea Lord: thou knowest that I love thee. He said unto him, Feed my lambs. He said to him again the second time, Simon, son of

Jonas, lovest thou me? He said unto him,
Yea, Lord: thou knowest that I love thee.
He said unto him. Feed my sheep. He said
unto him the third time, Simon, son lovest
thou me? Peter grieved because he said unto
him the third time, Lovest thou me? And
he said unto him, Lord, thou knowest all
things; thou knowest that I love thee. Jesus
said unto him, "Feed my sheep" (St. John
21:15a-17).

After telling Peter other things pertaining
to his death, He said unto him to "Follow
Me." Peter turned, seeing John following
him, and said to "Jesus, Lord, and what shall
this man do? Jesus said unto him, "If I will
that he tarry till I come, what is that to thee?
Follow thou me"(St John 21:18-22).

I must remember that this is a personal/
individual call. No one else can run my race.
The race is not given to the swift or the
strong, but to him that endure to the end. I
have to move on in what I have been called
to do. It's time to move on.

CHAPTER 4

BE CAREFUL OF FAULTFINDING

Faults are described as being guilty of wrong doing. The first faultfinder was Satan. He tried to find fault with the Most High God. In fact, he thought that he could do better than God, and set out to take over heaven (Isaiah 14:12-14). What he forgot was, you can not defeat your creator.

What did Satan do after he was kicked out of heaven? He started to create havoc here on earth. He started with the first family, Adam and Eve. He asked Eve (not Adam), "Has God said you shall not eat of every tree of the garden? And the woman said to the serpent, we may eat of the fruit of the trees of the garden: But of the tree which is in the midst of the garden, God

21

have said, you shall not eat of it, neither shall you touch it, lest you die. And the serpent said unto the woman, you shall not surely die: For God does know that in the day you eat there of, then your eyes shall be opened, and you shall be as gods, knowing good and evil" (Genesis 3:1-5).

Satan basically accused God of not telling the truth. He started faultfinding here on earth. When God called Adam and said to him, "Where are you?" What did Adam tell God as to why they were hiding? "I heard thy voice in the garden, and I was afraid, because I was naked; and I hid myself." God said, "Who told you, that you were naked? Hast thou eaten of the tree, whereof I commanded you not to eat of?" (Genesis 3:9-13) Then Adam blamed Eve. Eve blamed the serpent.

Faultfinding is a sin. There's a punishment for sin. "For the wages of sin is death; but the gift of God is eternal life through Jesus Christ our Lord" (Romans 6:23). Satan got kicked out of heaven and was told that because of it, he would be sent to hell (Isaiah 14:15). The serpent was told that because of his beguiling Eve, he was cursed above all cattle and above all beast of the field, and would go upon his belly and dust shall you eat the days of your life (Genesis 3:14). God gave to both Adam and Eve their punishments. "So he drove out the man; and he placed at the east of the garden of Eden Cherubims, and a flaming sword which turned every way, to keep the way of the tree of life" (Genesis 3:24).

God is faithful. He gives many opportunities for change. He did not stop loving Adam and Eve. He gave them another chance. He gave Satan a time to reek havoc. He allowed him to put his plans into action, but also told him what the results would be.

The enemy will cause us to find fault with almost everything. We complain about our size, hair, facial features, shape, and height and skin color. From the beginning of time, God knew what was best for each of us. When He made your bone size and length, it was best for you. We are uniquely designed. If He went as far as to give each one of us our own fingerprints and DNA, our body design was no mistake. It's the enemy that causes us to find fault with ourselves, as well as others.

Man will always think that things should be different. Our color, hair, body shapes, and resilience are specially designed of the Lord. It is not a mistake. We were made to withstand, when others are giving up.

He created us in His image and likeness. We are uniquely designed. We are like beautiful flowers, different species, but flowers just the same. Even within the same species, there are different colors, shapes, sizes, and heights. All according to God's design. Our ministry is different one from another, yet it completes the divine will of the Father. A house is made up of different fabrics/materials. The foundation of concrete, wood, metals and a various mixtures. Other fabrics are put on that foundation to make the walls, windows, doors, and roofs. It takes all of these parts to complete the building. The same way, it takes all of God's creations to complete His plan.

The scribes and Pharisees brought unto Jesus a woman taken in adultery; and when they had set her in the midst, they said unto Him, "Master, this woman was taken in adultery, in the very act. Now Moses in the law commanded us, that such should be stoned: but what do you say?"

This they said, tempting Jesus, that they might have to accuse Him. But Jesus stooped down, and with His finger wrote on the ground, as though he heard them not. So when they continued asking him, he lifted himself and said unto them, "He without sin amongst you, let him first cast a stone at her." (John 8:7). And again he stooped down, and wrote on the ground. And they which heard it, being convicted by their own con-science, went out one by one, beginning at the eldest, even unto the last: and Jesus was left alone, with the woman standing in the midst" (St. John 8:3-9).

To cover our own shortcomings, we sometimes blame others. How many times have you blamed others, when things went wrong? Why is it so hard to admit our wrongs? It's the enemy in me that causes the problem. The more Christ we put inside, the less reign the enemy has. We must learn to admit our wrongs and stop finding faults with others.

CHAPTER 5

WHEN MORNING COMES

Morning represents light. Daylight is the worldly meaning. Its spiritual meaning is the coming into the knowledge of Christ in your life. This represents the change from living in darkness to living in the light of Christ.

In tribulation, morning means a breakthrough. After going through pain, agony and distress, morning is that peace that only the Lord can bring. In school, when you just don't get it, and finally reach that aha moment, that's morning. When you are having trouble with your children, constantly praying and God brings about a change, that's morning! That habit that you can't seem to overcome, and the Lord delivers you....well, that's morning.

Your morning may be different from mine. But whatever you are going though, when God gives you peace, that's your morning. The situation may not be over, but He gives you peace while He completes the process. That's morning!

When you are financially strapped, constantly worrying about how you are going to make ends meet, and you're begging the Lord to send a financial blessing, but instead He gives you peace in your spirit to wait, well, that's your morning!

You have neighbors that get on your nerves and you pray that they move out of the neighborhood. God sends you a word to pray for them instead of against them. The change starts in you, and then, suddenly, you can see the change in your neighbors, once again, that's morning. Change in thinking from negative to positive is morning.

Lot, Abraham's nephew, was happy to see morning as the angels grabbed their hands to lead them out of Sodom, before it was destroyed by fire (Genesis 19:15). Jacob had wrestled with an angel all night and would not let go until he blessed him, just before day break (Genesis 32:22-29). The four lepers in Samaria during the great famine, knew that they were going to die. The decision was whether by the town's people or the Syrians. They chose the camp of the Syrian. Instead, they found food, clothing, drink, tents, silver and gold, which they shared with the town's people (II Kings 6:25, 7:3-16). What a morning! The lepers moved from selfishness to selflessness. That's morning.

When someone you've been praying for accepts Christ, that's morning. A chance for a new beginning. "Likewise, I say unto you, there is joy in the presence of the angels of God over one sinner that repents" (Luke 15:10). "For his anger endureth but a moment, in his favor is life: weeping may endure but for a night, but joy cometh in the morning" (Psalms 30:5).

Even though morning comes, that doesn't mean that you will have no more nights in your life. In this earthly life, there will still be ups and downs. The Lord gives us a way of escape that we may be able to stand. It doesn't mean that once you have escaped, that your trials are over. No, you will continue to go through trials and tribulations as long as you live.

When we leave this old world and enter into our eternal home in glory, then our real morning will come.. When 'that morning' comes, there will be no need for anymore crying because with God, there will be nothing but joy! Then, and only then, will we enjoy morning forever with the Lord, for there will be no more nights.

CHAPTER 6

YOU CAN'T USE WORLDLY HELP FOR A SPIRITUAL WARFARE

There have been times in my life, when there seemed to be nowhere to turn. When I felt spiritually impotent. My prayer life seemed nonexistent. No one understood what I felt. When I told others what was going on, instead of listening and encouraging me, I would hear about their situations. After that kind of conversation, I felt bewildered.

It doesn't matter how you try to get comfort from others, the results are the same. When things are that way, know that your situation is of the Lord.

These are the times that the Lord wants you to totally depend on Him. There is no reason to tell anyone else. He want you to tell Him. Even though we are in the flesh, our warfare is spiritual. It takes God to pull down the strongholds in your life. He is the only one who can help us by "Casting down imaginations, and every high thing that exalt its self against the knowledge of God, bringing into captivity every thought unto obedience of Christ" (II Cor. 10:3-5).

Our spiritual authority comes from the Lord. The enemy has a way of getting in front of our blessing, by blinding our view with worldly thoughts. Because we cannot see the solution, we give up. "We are not wrestling against flesh and blood, but against principalities, powers and rulers of darkness of this world. Against spiritual wickedness in high places" (Ephesians 6:12).

We are to "Endure hardness, as a good soldier of Jesus Christ. No man that's at war, entangles himself with the affairs of this life, so that he may please him who hath chosen him to be a soldier." (II Timothy

2:3-4). When we go to the Lord with our problems, only He can give us the right answer. If you really want the truth, wait on Him. Pray for insight and He will give it to you. You may not get the answer through spiritual meditation, sometimes He sends it through someone.

Whether through spiritual thought or by a messenger in the form of a friend, child, stranger, neighbor, or family member, you will always know His voice when you hear it. Most times, the messenger does not know why he says what he has said. So don't dismiss the message, because of the messenger. The world cannot help in a spiritual warfare, only the Lord can.

CHAPTER 7

THE PRISONS OF LIFE

What prison are you in? Is your prison mental or physical? Whether mental or physical, while you are confined, make your mark on life. If you have no job, get busy around where you live. Paint your house, do yard work or re-organize your tools. Work in the garden. Clean the house, vacuum, dust, mop or wax. Get rid of things that you have no need of, and unnecessary clutter. Sew, write, and visit the nursing homes/hospitals. Just don't sit and wallow in the mire of your life. Do something! Make your stay a worthwhile tenure during your time here on earth.

Joseph, who was a dreamer, always saw himself in power over his brothers. He was a dreamer of power, until his siblings started to hate him. Not only was he talkative, but he was favored by his father, Jacob. Favored so much, that he was given a coat of many colors.

Jacob always sent Joseph to check on his brothers, as they attended the sheep. One day, when his father sent him to check on them, they were not in the area where they normally were. He finally found them, after asking someone. They saw him before he got to them. They said, 'Here comes the dreamer. Let's kill him.' Reuben, the oldest brother, talked them out of killing him by telling them to put him into a pit (Gen. 37:3-22).

While sitting beside the pit, having lunch, they decided to sell him to some Ishmeelites, on their way to Egypt (Gen. 37:28). Joseph was sold to Potiphar, an officer of Pharaoh, captain of the guard.

Joseph prospered in Egypt, because the Lord was with him. He found grace in his master's sight (Gen. 39:1-4a). Always remember, when you start to being blessed, the enemy will attack. The enemy came in the form of Potiphar's wife. When you resist the devil, the Bible said, he will flee from you (James4:7). Sometimes the fleeing have to be done by you. When you find yourself in a situation that can cause havoc, run! Don't be ashamed, run as fast as you can. Joseph ran! But he was still accused and put into prison (Gen. 39:20).

In prison, Joseph was promoted to be in control of other prisoners. When the Lord have plans for your life, it doesn't matter where you are, He will bless you. It doesn't matter what the world may try to do to you, the Lord will bless you while you are in your mess. Joseph, 'the dreamer,' became the interpreter for other dreamers, the chief butler, the baker and later, Pharoah (Gen. 40:2,8, 41:16). Joseph was seventeen, when he was sold and thirty, when Pharoah set him over the land of Egypt (Gen.

37:2,41:41,46). Joseph never took credit for the gift of interpretation of dreams. He knew, of himself, he could do nothing. Only to the Lord was the credit due.

Joseph's brothers were sent to Egypt to buy food because of the famine. Joseph, after finding out that his father and brother Benjamin were well, made himself known to his brothers. He told them not to worry nor be angry with themselves for selling him. God had sent him before them to preserve their lives (Gen. 45:3-5).

In spite of how things may seem, God's plan will be carried out. No matter what may have you bound, it's only temporary. Whether physical or spiritually, the Master has a plan of redemption. Seek Him for the answer on everything, and discover true freedom.

CHAPTER 8

YOUR HOLE IS NEVER TOO DEEP FOR GOD

Your hole may not always be physical. It may be spiritual. When you are at your lowest point in your life, that's your hole. Sometimes your hole can be your marriage, your job, your children, or your neighbors. There's one thing that will keep you in your hole and that's being unforgiving. Whoever you are angry with or blame for things that have gone wrong in your life, forgive them and go on! Sometimes that someone is yourself.

Both Joseph and Daniel were thrown in a physical pit/den. However, the spiritual man inside of them was not in a hole. They both knew God, and never stop praying.

Joseph, because of his purpose, was not delivered right away. It took about thirteen years before he came into the fullness of his purpose (Gen. 37:24-28).

Daniel was delivered instantly. You see, the Lord locked the lion's jaws, even though he had to stay there over night (Daniel 6:5-23).

You see, the Lord allows things to happen to us, to 'promote growth.' The things we plant come up. That old saying, 'You reap what you sow,' is true. You sow happiness and happiness grows. Sow anger and anger will grow.

Before you plant, you must prepare the soil. The weeds must be dug up and the hard soil softened. The weeding is the changing of your worldly deeds and accepting Jesus Christ. You see, Jesus is the fertilizer that you mix with your soil. What happens when you just dig a hole and drop seeds in the midst of weeds? The weeds will choke out your seeds. Even when you prepare the soil, you will still have weeds. Don't let them take over. Pull up all the weeds and water the plant, to promote growth.

For most of us, as children, the ground of our lives was prepared by our parents. Seeds were planted and watered. As we got out on our own, we stopped weeding, watering and fertilizing. But the good thing is that our parents and others continued to pray for us. So when we fall in the hole, pit or den of our lives, we cry out to Jesus. He hears us and comes to our rescue. You see, even the prettiest, sweetish smelling rose, has thorns.

The holes bring us closer to the Lord. Even though we sometimes don't know He's there, He is! He is true to His word (Hebrew 5: 6)(Genesis 28:15). Things just don't happen to us by chance. Some things we bring upon ourselves and others are by the divine will of God.

Like Abraham and Sarah, we know the plan, but it's not happening as fast as we think it should, so we try to help God out. Like Rebekah, when she was pregnant, she was having a difficult time and inquired of the Lord. He told her that two nations were warring within her. The eldest would serve the younger one. So she started out to make that happen (Genesis 25:20-28, 27: 1).

The most important thing to remember, when you are in your hole, is that worship and praise will bring you out. We seem to think that crying, complaining and having 'a pity party,' is the answer. It takes a long time to move out of your circumstances, when you complain. Start praising and things will happen. The man with the unclean spirits, when he saw Jesus, worshiped Him. It was after his worship, that he was set free (Mark 5: 2, 6). No weapons formed against us shall prosper (Isaiah 54:17). So praise and pray, praise and pray some more, and Jesus will deliver you out of the holes of your life.

CHAPTER 9

DELAY IS NOT DENIAL

Things don't always come when we ask for them. Some time the wait is so long, that you start to feel as if you're not going to get them. When that happens, what do you do? Do you give up or do you keep waiting? Or maybe we get like Sarah and decide to help God out.

As Christians/ believers, we must trust Jesus because He's true to His word. Jesus told His disciples, as He prepared them for His crucifixion, "Verily, verily, I say unto you, He that believe in me, the works that I do shall he do also; and greater works than these shall he do, because I go to my Father.

"And what so ever you shall ask in my name, that will I do, that the Father maybe glorified in the Son. If you shall ask anything in my name, I will do it. If you love me, keep my commandments (St. John 14:12-15)."

Let's get one thing straight. As a Christian, you don't ask for just anything. Just in case you're not sure, here's some no-nos. Don't ask Jesus to give you someone else's husband or wife. Don't ask for someone else's possessions.

When you have the mind of Christ, you ask for those things that are acceptable to Him.

When Daniel prayed for the answer to a vision, it didn't come right away. The answer was held up for twenty-one days by the enemy (Prince of the Kingdom of Persia). God had sent the answer by Gabriel, and for twenty-one days, the enemy withstood him. But, Michael came to help (Daniel 10:2, 10-14).

The delay is not always because He's making us wait, but the enemy gets in the way. Don't give up! Hold on. Help is on the way!

David was anointed king when Saul was rejected by God, but did not begin to reign until after Saul died (I Samuel 16:12-13). Imagine being anointed to be king and continuing to care for your father's sheep! Remember, what God has in store for you, will surely come to pass.

CHAPTER 10

I CAN'T HELP, BUT I CAN GIVE YOU A REFERRAL

I have spent most of my life being helpful. At least 'I thought' I was being helpful. You see, God gave me a spirit of helping, along with several other gifts. Sometime we believe because we have been given a gift, we are to use it for any and everyone.

In the beginning, we do things that are natural for us to do. It's like breathing. Because it's in me, when I see a need, I rush to fulfill it. Some one has to do it, so I step up.

Over the years I have found myself helping without being asked. Sometimes the person may not have wanted my help. As the years passed, I realized that I am only to help if I'm asked and/told to do so by the spirit. The Lord have let me know that I have been a hindrance, rather than a help. Because it was so natural for me to help, the ones I helped returned again, and again. What once was a joy, became a chore.

You will find that people will take advantage of your kindness. If you are the kind of person that's willing to give or to help, some will try to make it your responsibility. Brother Carter, before he became a Christian, would use the saying, 'Find a sucker, bump his head.' Meaning— when you find someone that you can take advantage of, use him until you can't use him any more (Or, like Bill Wither's Song, use him until you use him up).

God gives us gifts to help build the Kingdom and instructs us when to do so. When we mature spiritually, we use them as needed. We are to exercise our gifts. When you love to do a particular thing, we must; (1) practice to enhance that gift, (2) exercise it at every opportunity and (3) use it for experience. When you become proficient in that area, then your talent can be used to make a living.

God wants to use us for His Kingdom work down here on earth. You have been prepared for the work that you are to do. "Before I formed thee in the belly I knew thee; and before thou came forth out of the womb I sanctified thee, and I ordained thee a prophet unto the nations" (Jeremiah 1:5). "I can do all things through Christ, which strengthened me (Philippians 4:13).

We are to use our gifts as God directs us. When we step out on our own...we are getting the glory and people keep returning for our help. What God really wants us to do, is to refer them to Him. Had Peter and John not given the credit to Jesus, when they told the lame man that laid at the gate of the temple called Beautiful, he would have praised them.

But Peter said, "Silver and gold have I none; but such as I have give I thee: In the name of Jesus Christ of Nazareth, rise up and walk. And he took him by the right hand, and lifted him up: and immediately his feet and ankle bones received strength. And he leaping up stood, and walked, and entered with them into the temple, walking and leaping, and praising God" (Acts 3:2-8).

We can do nothing of ourselves. As we use the gifts that God has given us, we should let people know that it is Him and not ourselves, that deserve all the praise.

Paul and Silas were beaten and thrown into prison for casting out a spirit of divination from a young lady, when she could no longer make money for her master. Paul and Silas were taken to the rulers in the market place. While they were in prison, with their feet in stocks, they prayed at midnight and sang praises to God; and the prisoners heard them. Suddenly there was a great earthquake, so that the foundation of the prison was shaken: and immediately all the doors were opened, everyone's bands were loosed (Acts 16:18-26).

There is no prisons, problems or any other issues that God cannot solve. Even Jesus referred to His Father as His source..."Believest thou not that I am in the Father, and the Father in me? The words that I speak unto you, I speak not of myself: but the Father that dwelleth in me, he doeth the works. He that loveth me not keepeth not my sayings: and the word which you hear is not mine, but the Father's which sent me" (John 14:10,24). We can do nothing of ourselves. Take no credit for the blessings that others may receive through you. Always remember, the gift is no good without the giver. Instead of taking credit for a good deed or need, refer them to Jesus.

CHAPTER 11

WE ARE WINNERS

J ust imagine how we would live our lives, if we knew we would never lose. We would never give trouble a second thought. Neither would we worry about the outcome of any situation.

We have been promised victory in Christ Jesus. Jesus told his disciples, "Behold, I give unto you power to tread on serpents and scorpions, and over all the power of the enemy: and nothing shall by any means hurt you" (Luke 10:19). Don't forget, "If you shall ask anything in my name, I will do it" (St. John 14:14).

We live defeated lives, because we have doubt. Lack of faith is a sin. We use words, such as, "I hope so," "I'm not sure," and "Maybe." When we were chasing or running out in the world, we believed we could do almost anything. There wasn't anything that I set my mind to that I didn't accomplish.

It's amazing how our thinking changed when we became Christians. We accepted Christ in our lives, realizing that it was Him that allowed us to do the things that we did. But now we become cautious. We are afraid to take chances. We really should have more confidence, not less, as Christians.

We have a written warranty that tell us about the product. The Maker guarantees the performance and the results for His users (us). All we need to do is follow the directions. If we are following Christ's instruction/footsteps, get ready for things to happen! No runner, swimmer, bicyclist or race car driver, can see the outcome before it happens. But through faith, they believe they are winners. We are victorious! We are winners forever through Christ Jesus!

CHAPTER 12

SEASONS IN OUR LIVES

According to the American Heritage School Dictionary, seasons are the natural division of the year–spring, summer, autumn and winter. In our lives, seasons represent change or growth; time to become different. Our seasons of maturation each represent a period of time. First, there is infancy–a time of being a baby, then a toddler. Next, there are stages of growth called Childhood. Adolescence–the period between youth and maturity—is the next period. The period between physical and psychological development that leads from childhood to adulthood takes about 21 years. Adulthood is the time or condition of being fully grown or developed, having maturity.

"To everything there is a season, and a time to every purpose under the heaven: A time to be born, and a time to die; a time to plant and a time to pluck up that which is planted. A time to kill and a time to heal; a time to break down and a time to build up; A time to weep, and a time to laugh; a time to mourn, and a time to dance; A time to cast away stones, and a time to gather stones together; A time to embrace, and a time to refrain from embracing; A time to get, and a time to lose; A time to keep, and a time to cast away; A time to rend, and a time to sew; A time to keep silence, and a time to speak; A time to love, and a time to hate; A time of war, and a time of peace" (Ecclesiastes 3: 1-8).

From the beginning, God set up seasons. Why do seasons come? Seasons and change promote growth. There would be no need for change, if everything were perfect. Jesus was the only perfect man. "Jesus Christ, the same yesterday, and today and forever" (Hebrews 13:8). "For I am the Lord, I change not; therefore ye sons of Jacob are not consumed" (Malachi 3:6).

When we reach the time in our lives that we have completed the work that God has ordained here on earth, there will be no need for any more changes. Our physical body will die, but our spiritual being will live forever. For those of us who sometimes think we are perfect, this should explain why we are still here. The perfected, completed body will die. We will have served our purpose.

The righteousness we have is of self. "As it is written, there is none righteous, no not one" (Romans 3:10). As we grow from one stage to another, there should be some evidence of change.

What would you think if a school-age child was still being breast fed? Or if a school-age child still had no teeth. Something would be wrong! God has set things up where everything has a time and a season. There are some that, even though their body grows, they try to remain the same. In fact, they don't want to mature.

But one only has to look at nature. The flowers have their seasons. It doesn't matter how beautiful they maybe, how much you water and fertilize, the blooms, after a few days, still die. Like plants, there's a budding time in our lives. An opening time, a full bloom, a withering time and a dying time. "And as it is appointed unto men once to die, but after this, the judgment" (Hebrews 9:28). Make the most out of the different seasons in your life. Don't try to stay where you no longer belong. Seize each moment as if it's your last, because the end will certainly come.

CHAPTER 13

NO VISUAL MEANS
OF SUPPORT

I know most of us have seen shows on television, where a magician causes a person to rise above a table. A ring is taken, like a hoop, and pulled over the body to show that nothing is above or below to hold them up.

When Moses asked Pharaoh to let God's people go, he wouldn't. Aaron was instructed to throw down his rod and it became a serpent. The magicians did the same and their rods became serpents, also. But Aaron's rod swallowed up their rods. A 'now you see it, and now you don't' situation. Imitators! God, being a spirit, we can not really see how or what He is going to do.

We are 'show me' people. If someone tells you they are going to give you something (money), we really don't believe it until we see it. A 'believe it or not' situation.

We treat God the same way. "I know He said it, but when? Will I have it by the date I need it? I know He works through people. I wonder who He will send it through?"

We spend most of our time trying to figure out the mechanics of it all.

We have past history that reveals what God can do. Moses, with the children of Israel at the Red Sea, when they saw Pharaoh, they were afraid. They cried out unto the Lord. They accused Moses of bringing them into the wilderness to die. Moses told them, "Fear not, stand still and see the salvation of the Lord, which he will show you today...for the Egyptians whom you have seen today, you shall see no more forever. The Lord shall fight for you, and you shall hold your peace" (Exodus 14:10-11,

13-14). The Red Sea was divided and they went over on dry ground.

Daniel in the lion's den: The Lord did not stop them from putting him in the den. His plan was greater than that. He shut the lion's mouth (Daniel 6: 16-21). Shadrach, Mesheck and Abednego in the fiery furnace: God did not stop the process, but was there in the furnace with them (Daniel 3:16-27). God's plan cannot always be understood, but the results are miraculous. Both Daniel and his friends, trusted God to do the impossible, although they could not fore see the outcome.

All the 'woes' of Job: He didn't understand why things were happening, but he never blamed God. After losing everything, Job was blessed with more than before (Job 4: 12-13).

We want to know or see how things are going to work out. When Jesus fed the five thousand with two fishes and five loaves of bread, the disciples didn't understand how He was going to feed everyone, but followed His instructions. All these are miracles that could not be performed by man (Luke 9:13-17).

Peter and John's healing of the lame man was past the understanding of the one healed (Act 3: 1-9).

Think back to times in your life when you couldn't see your way out, but God stepped in and made a way. There is a window of time that we have, when action need to be taken at that moment, or you will miss your opportunity. Have you noticed that at certain times, so much is going on in your life that you are running here and there? People are requiring things from you. You are up early and staying up late. You really have no time to relax. Then all of a sudden, things slow down. If they slow down too much, you become bored.

When God gives you that break, use it! Do things that you haven't had the time to finish. Spend time with the Father, asking for directions. Let Him tell you what, how and when to do things. When He gives it to you, don't put it off. Your window of opportunity might close. Trust Him! Know that what has been promised, will come to pass.

The enemy doesn't want you to succeed. He wants you to fail. He brings about doubt. How is God going to do this? What if He doesn't? When doubt starts to cloud your mind, remember, "God is not a man that he can lie; neither the son of man, that he should repent; has he said, and shall he not do it? Or has he spoken, and shall he not make it good" (Numbers 23: 19)?

"Paul, a servant of God, and apostle of Jesus Christ, according to the faith of God's elect, and acknowledging of the truth which is after godliness. In hope of eternal life, which God, that cannot lie, promised before the world began" (Titus 1: 1-2). We must remember that He can not lie. What He promised will happen.

He has given us power to perform all the things that we need to complete our assigned duties. "Behold, I give unto you power to tread on serpents and scorpions, and over all the power of the enemy: and nothing shall by any means hurt you" (Luke 10:19).

Don't let the enemy steal your promises that God has given, nor give them away.

Even though we can't see how it's going to take place, know that it will surely come to pass. "If you shall ask anything in my name, I will do it" (St. John 14:14). "Trust in the Lord with all your heart and lean not unto your own understanding, in all your ways acknowledge him and he shall direct your path" (Proverb 3:5-6).

We are in similar times that were in the days of Noah, before the flood. "The earth also was corrupt before God, and the earth filled with violence" (Genesis 6: 11). The world was in a wicked state.

Likewise, wickedness seems to be today's life style. In spite of what we see with our eyes, what we see with our spiritual mind, is that God has the plan secure. This is by no surprise to God. He has a divine person to carry out/on His plan.

Don't let the enemy block the vision that has been set before you. Keep your eyes on the prize of the high calling of God. Don't stop praising the Father! It can only go the way that He allows.

What we see today is not new! It's just a repeat performance of the past. Remember, our lives are in the hand of God. Pray for guidance and keep moving forward. We may not see what's ahead, but God does.

www.ingramcontent.com/pod-product-compliance
Lightning Source LLC
LaVergne TN
LVHW011215080426
835508LV00007B/796